O<small>N A</small> U.S. tal
asked what
that Barack Oba_n.  .... born in Kenya.
"Pah!" I replied (or words to that effect). "Your
president was plainly born in Brussels."

American conservatives have struggled to
press President Obama's policies into a meaningful narrative. Is he a socialist? Not exactly,
at least not in the traditional sense of wanting
the state to own key industries. Is he, as
Dinesh D'Souza argues, actuated by the 1950s
anticolonialism of his absent, but idealized,
father? Perhaps, but in domestic terms, this
doesn't take us very far. Is he then a straight-
forward New Deal big spender, in the model
of FDR and LBJ? Up to a point.

What all these interpretations have in
common is that they seek to define the president in American terms. But looking across
from my side of the Atlantic, there seems to
be a much simpler explanation. President
Obama wants to Europeanize America. All
right, he wouldn't put it in those terms, partly
because the electorate wouldn't wear it and

partly because he sees himself as less Euro-centric than any of his 43 predecessors.

My guess is that if anything, Obama would verbalize his ideology using the same vocabulary that Eurocrats do. He would say he wants a fairer America, a more tolerant America, a less arrogant America, a more engaged America. When you prize away the cliché, what these phrases amount to are higher taxes, less patriotism, a bigger role for state bureaucracies, and a transfer of sovereignty to global institutions. In other words, President Obama wants to make the U.S. more like the EU.

He is not pursuing a set of random initiatives lashed arbitrarily together but a program of comprehensive Europeanization: European health care, European welfare, European carbon taxes, European day care, European college education, even a European foreign policy, based engagement with supranational technocracies, nuclear disarmament, and a reluctance to deploy forces overseas.

No previous president has offered such uncritical support for European integration.

It's hardly surprising that Obama should be such an enthusiast for a European superstate: He is building his own version at home.

On his very first trip to Europe as president, Obama declared, "In my view, there is no Old Europe or New Europe. There is a united Europe." Having silkily dispensed with the old Rumsfeldian idea that the U.S. should deal with EU states as individual nations, he went on to dismiss the Euroskeptic majorities in most European countries: "I believe in a strong Europe, and a strong European Union, and my administration is committed to doing everything we can to support you."

It's hardly surprising that Obama should be such an enthusiast for a European superstate: He is building his own version at home.

The critical difference between the European and American unions has to do with the location of power. The foundational doctrine of the U.S. was that decisions should be decentralized for the people they affect. The framers had seen firsthand what happened when power was concentrated and were determined to keep their rulers in check. The EU had precisely the opposite foundational imperative. Its patriarchs, scarred by the experience of the Second World War, were determined to merge their nations, to centralize power, and to ensure that decisions were vested in the hands of neutral experts who didn't need to worry about public opinion.

The preoccupations of the two sets of founding fathers are visible in the debates that surrounded their charters, as well as in the documents themselves. The U.S. Constitution is concerned with the diffusion and democratization of power. The EU Treaties, by contrast, commit their signatories, in Article 1, to establish "an ever-closer union." The U.S. Constitution, with all its amendments, is

7,200 words long. The EU Constitution, now formally known as the Lisbon Treaty, is 76,000. The U.S. Constitution concerns itself with broad principles, such as the balance between state and federal authorities. The EU Constitution busies itself with such minutiae as space exploration, the rights of disabled people, and the status of asylum seekers. The U.S. Constitution, in particular the Bill of Rights, is mainly about the liberty of the individual. The EU Constitution is mainly about the power of the state.

Here is the categorical difference between the two unions, the elemental distinction of which all the other differences are aspects. Because the U.S. was designed along what we might loosely term Jeffersonian lines, it has tended to have a small government, strong local authorities, a flourishing private sphere, a limited welfare system, relatively low taxes, and skepticism toward global technocracies. The EU, having been conceived around the concept of an ever-closer union, tends the opposite way.

I don't doubt the sincerity of those Americans who want to copy the European model. A few may be snobs who wear their Euro-enthusiasm as a badge of sophistication. But

---

The U.S. Constitution is mainly about the liberty of the individual. The EU Constitution is mainly about the power of the state.

---

most genuinely believe that making their country less American, more like the rest of the world, would make it more comfortable and peaceable. All right, growth would be slower, but the quality of life might improve. All right, taxes would be higher, but workers need no longer fear sickness or unemployment. All right, the U.S. would no longer be the world's superpower, but perhaps that would make it more popular. Is a European future truly so terrible?

Yes. Take it from me, my friends. I have been an elected Member of the European Parliament (MEP) for 11 years. I have seen firsthand what the European political model means. I inhabit your future – or at least the future toward which your current rulers seem intent on taking you. Before you follow us, let me tell you a few things about it.

Why Americans Are Richer Than Europeans

Many Americans, and many Europeans, have a collective memory of how Europeans managed to combine economic growth with social justice. Didn't Western Europe do tremendously well after the Second World War? Wasn't its success associated with something called "Rhineland capitalism" or "the social market"? (This latter phrase calls to mind F. A. Hayek's observation that "Social is a weasel word that has acquired the power to empty the nouns it qualifies of their meanings.")

Like most folk memories, the idea of a European economic miracle has some basis in fact. Between 1945 and 1974, Western Europe did indeed outperform the U.S. And in retrospect, we can see why. Europe happened to enjoy perfect conditions for rapid growth. Infrastructure had been destroyed during the war, but an educated, industrious, and disciplined workforce remained. There was also, for the first time in Europe's history, mass migration. Within individual nations, people moved in unprecedented numbers from the countryside to the growing cities. Within Europe, they journeyed from the Mediterranean littoral to the coalfields and steelworks of northern Europe. And millions more came from beyond Europe – from North Africa, Turkey, and the former British, French, and Dutch colonies.

As if all these advantages were not enough, Europe received a massive external stimulus. Thirteen billion dollars were disbursed through the Marshall Plan between 1948 and

1952, on top of the $12 billion already given by the U.S. in aid since the end of the war. Colossal as these transfers were by the standards of the time, Europe was receiving an even more valuable gift in the form of the U.S. security guarantee. The defense budgets of most Western European states were, as a percentage of gross domestic product, around a quarter of that of the U.S. (Britain and France were exceptions.) The money that was freed up by low military spending could be spent instead on civil programs.

In those circumstances, it would have been extraordinary had Europe *not* prospered. Human nature being what it is, however, few European leaders attributed their success to the fact that they were recovering from an artificial low, still less to external assistance. They convinced themselves, rather, that they were responsible for their countries' growth rates. Their genius, they thought, lay in having hit upon a European "third way" between the excesses of American capitalism and the totalitarianism of Soviet communism.

They believed in markets, but regulated markets. Instead of the industrial strife that they had experienced before the war, they would establish a tripartite system in which employers, labor unions, and government officials worked together. Instead of seesawing between Left and Right, they would have consensual coalition governments in which both Christian Democrats and Social Democrats accepted the broad framework of a mixed social market. Instead of competition between states, they would pursue political and economic integration.

We can now see where that road leads: to burgeoning bureaucracy, more spending, higher taxes, slower growth, and rising unemployment. But an entire political class has grown up believing not just in the economic superiority of Euro-corporatism but in its moral superiority. After all, if the American system were better – if people and businesses could thrive without government supervision – there would be less need for politicians. As

Upton Sinclair once observed, "It is difficult to get a man to understand something when his job depends on not understanding it."

Nonetheless, the economic data are pitilessly clear. For the past 40 years, Europeans have fallen further and further behind Americans in their standard of living. In 1974, Western Europe, defined as the 15 members of the EU prior to the admission of the former Communist countries in 2004, accounted for 36 percent of world GDP. Today that figure is 26 percent. In 2020 it will be 15 percent. In the same period, the U.S. share of world GDP has remained, and is forecast to remain, fairly steady at around 26 percent.

At the same time, Europe has become accustomed to a high level of structural un-employment. Indeed, if we exclude the United Kingdom, the EU failed to produce a single net private-sector job between 1980 and 1992. Only now, as the U.S. applies a European-style economic strategy based on fiscal stimulus, nationalization, bailouts, quantitative easing, and the regulation of private-sector remuneration, has the rate of unemployment in the U.S. leaped to European levels.

Some EU leaders privately recognize that the U.S. economy is more dynamic than their

---

For the past 40 years, Europeans have fallen further and further behind Americans in their standard of living.

---

own, and they occasionally issue staccato statements to the effect that they really ought to do something about it. In 2000, for example, they committed themselves to something called the Lisbon Agenda, designed to give the EU "the most competitive and dynamic knowledge-based economy in the world, capable of sustainable economic growth with

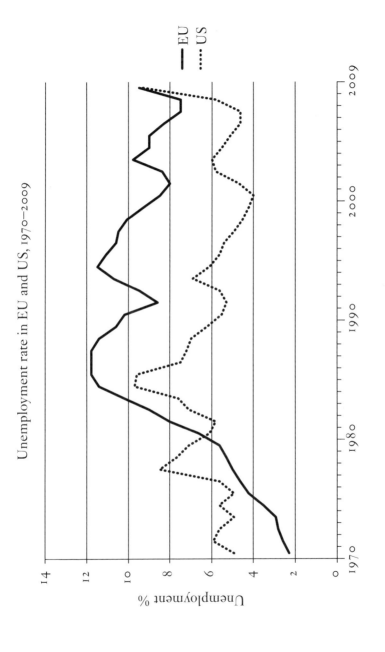

Unemployment rate in EU and US, 1970–2009

more and better jobs and greater social cohesion, and respect for the environment by 2010." To which it is tempting to remark, as Sarah Palin might put it, How's that working out for y'all?

Then again, no one ever really believed that the Lisbon Agenda would have much impact in the real world. It was intended in the spirit of one of those Soviet slogans about higher production: a Stakhanovite statement of intent.

The French philosopher René Descartes famously imagined that everything we thought we could see was in fact being manipulated by a malicious demon who controlled our senses. Eurocrats evidently see themselves in the role of that demon. The EU they describe is one of high growth, full democracy, and growing global influence. But this EU exists only in European Commission communiqués, in European Council press releases, in European Parliament resolutions.

European legislation has become declamatory: a way to "send a message" or to show that the people passing it care very much about a subject. It is no longer expected to connect with the real world.

I have lost count of how many times I have had variants of the following conversation with my fellow MEPs or with Commission officials:

Hannan: "We have a serious problem with unemployment."

Eurocrat: "Nonsense. Look at the resolution we adopted last month. The fight against unemployment is one of our top three priorities."

Hannan: "Yes, but our regulations on working hours, statutory works councils, paternity leave, and temporary workers are deterring employers from taking people on."

Eurocrat: "Didn't you hear what I just said, Hannan? One of our *top three priorities!*"

Not all EU leaders engage in self-deception, of course. Many of them concede that taking everything together, the American economy is stronger and more dynamic than their own. But this, they tell themselves, is a price well worth paying for Europe's quality of life. A European worker enjoys more leisure than his American counterpart, they argue, with shorter working days and longer vacations. He has a proper two-hour lunch, instead of gobbling a sandwich at his desk. He has time to play with his children.

This is certainly true. It now takes four Germans to put in the same number of man-hours as three Americans: the average German works 1,350 hours a year to the American's 1,800.

The EU as a whole has adopted a statutory maximum working week of 48 hours. Some member states have gone further. In France, for example, workers are prohibited from working for more than 35 hours a week.

In the short term, all this is very pleasant. Long vacations, paternity leave, a high minimum wage, a short working week: What's not to like? The trouble is that eventually, the money runs out. Europe is falling further and further behind, sustaining its living standards by borrowing, dwindling as a force in the world. The U.S., which has expanded its federal government by 30 percent since 2008, seems determined to duplicate that error.

Repealing State Health Care: If It Were Done When 'Tis Done, Then 'Twere Well It Were Done Quickly

Once ObamaCare takes hold, it won't easily be undone. The moment politicians become responsible for treating the sick, it becomes almost impossible to suggest any significant overhaul of the system – or indeed, any reduction in the budget.

I can best demonstrate this phenomenon with a personal recollection. In August 2009, I was asked on Fox News whether I'd recommend the British health care model to Americans. I replied that if you look at international comparators, Britain fared badly. Our waiting times were longer than in other Western nations and our survival rates lower. Britain was pretty much the last place in the industrialized world where you'd want to be diagnosed with cancer, stroke, or heart disease.

This wasn't because of any failing on the part of our medical professionals, I said. Many wonderful people became doctors and nurses because they wanted to help others. But the system didn't maximize their potential. Unlike most European health care systems, where there is a mix of state and private provision, the British system is monolithic: Everything is run by the government and funded out of general taxation. Governments, as we know, don't run things terribly well. They weren't very good at building cars, operating airlines, or installing telephones, and they're not much better at managing hospitals.

The British National Health Service (NHS), I added, was the third-largest employer in the world behind the People's Liberation Army in China and Indian Railways, employing 1.3 million people. Yet the doctors and nurses were a minority within that 1.3 million: They were outnumbered by administrative and other nonmedical staff.

I joked that simply to say what I was saying would open me to attacks in Britain. I would be accused of "insulting our hardworking doctors and nurses." It didn't take long for my jocular prediction to be fulfilled. A few days after my return to the U.K., Labour politicians went into overdrive. It was "unpatriotic," said then Health Minister Andy Burnham, to criticize the NHS in front of a foreign audience. Then Prime Minister Gordon Brown dedicated a passage of his speech to the Labour conference to excoriating me. The main Labour newspaper, the *Daily Mirror*, trotted out the very cliché that I had forecast: I had, it said, "insulted our hardworking doctors and nurses."

Not only is calling for significant reform unacceptable, so is wanting to constrain the budget. Once ministers become responsible for bodies lying on trolleys in corridors for want of a bed, it becomes impossible – morally as well as politically – to withhold funding. Every British department is now facing budget reductions of, on average, 19 percent, but the health care budget was specially exempted from the cuts in a pre-election promise and will continue to grow.

Nigel Lawson, Margaret Thatcher's chancellor of the exchequer, wrote after leaving office:

> *The National Health Service is the closest thing the English have to a religion, with those who practice in it regarding themselves as a priesthood. This made it quite extraordinarily difficult to reform. For a bunch of laymen, who called themselves the Government, to presume to tell the priesthood that they must change their ways in any respect whatever was clearly intolerable. And faced with a dispute between their priests and ministers, the public would have no hesitation in taking the part of the priesthood.*

Britain thus finds itself in a paradoxical situation. Every day, the newspapers carry horror stories about what happens in hospitals. We read of people traveling abroad for treatment, of thousands of deaths from infections picked up in wards, of potentially lifesaving drugs being withheld on grounds of cost rationing.

The one thing certain to be bigger and more remote than a big and remote insurance company is the federal government.

Yet no one is allowed to suggest a connection between these outcomes and the system that produces them. Do that, and you're "insulting our hardworking doctors and nurses."

Privately, of course, many doctors and nurses believe that the NHS needs a fundamental overhaul. Following my Fox interview – which, partly because it fell during the August "silly season," was the leading news story in the U.K. – I received two sorts of e-mails: those from people who agreed and who often recounted horror stories of their own; and those that asserted that I was a heartless Tory who wanted poor people to be left to die "as happens in America." While there were several NHS administrators in the latter camp, most of the doctors I heard from were in the former.

For what it's worth, I think there are ways in which the U.S. could usefully improve its health care system. The current setup, partly because of the costs of litigation, is more expensive than it needs to be and gives too much power to the insurance companies. But the one thing certain to be bigger and more remote than a big and remote insurance company is the federal government.

You don't have to be a Democrat to fret about the uninsured in America. You don't have to be a think-tank specialist to come up with better alternatives. You don't have to be an angry populist to feel that the system of litigation, which forces doctors to take out expensive insurance against lawsuits – and to pass the costs on to their patients – needs reform. But reform should be approached within the spirit of the U.S. Constitution: with the citizen, rather than the government, taking charge, and respecting the jurisdiction of the 50 states.

Instead, in March 2010, the U.S. opted for a federal role in directing health care. Not, that is, a federal role in paying for those who would otherwise be unable to afford treatment, but a state-administered system. True, the government option will initially sit alongside private schemes. But this is how state health care began in Canada. After a while, ministers found that, having assumed responsibility for the system, they were more or less obliged to keep expanding it at the expense of the private sector. After a while, the Canadian health care system was close to being a state monopoly, with private insurance almost squeezed out.

The U.S. is not Canada, of course, and the system adopted by the Obama administration is not the same as either the British or Canadian models. But the principle has now been established that there will be a government-run provision – not simply as a safety net for the poor but also as a direct competitor to private alternatives. The system will be funded out of general taxation, with practitioners answering to state officials. I really hope you've thought this through, my friends. Because believe me, once it beds down, there will be no going back.

Coercing Virtue: The Long-Term Impact of Euro-welfare

The expansion of the state in Europe hasn't just reduced economic growth. More damagingly, it has squeezed out personal morality. As taxes have risen, charitable donations have fallen: The average European gives $80 to charity each year, the average American $300.

Euro-sophists believe that there is something intrinsically immoral about the American system because it fails the destitute. This failure is inferred from the relatively low benefit entitlements received by poor Americans and from the conditionality of welfare payments. It is a stock phrase of virtually every European politician, regardless of party, that "a society is judged by how it treats the worst off." Plainly, then, there must be something selfish – and possibly also racist – about a people who keep voting for a system that treats the neediest so pitilessly.

It rarely occurs to critics that there might be better ways to measure the efficacy of a welfare state than by the size of its budget. Indeed, in a truly successful social security system, budgets ought to fall over time as former recipients are lifted into better and more productive lives.

This, of course, was the original rationale for welfare. But it has been almost entirely forgotten in Europe, where dependency has become structural. Benefits that were intended to have a one-off, transformative effect have instead become permanent, as recipients arrange their affairs around qualifying for subventions. Millions have become trapped in the squalor of disincentives and low expectations. In Britain, which is by no means as badly off as many EU members, the annual welfare budget, including the lump-sum payments that, as in the U.S., are called "tax credits," comes to more than $500 billion a year. Yet this huge contribution has little impact on either poverty or inequality.

It's the same story elsewhere in Europe: Paying people to be poor has created more and more poor people.

The U.S. is different, and different for reasons that again can be traced back to the DNA encoded at Philadelphia.

In 1996, President Clinton signed into law a reform package that had been proposed by the Republicans in Congress. It stands as the only meaningful overhaul of social security anywhere in the world, succeeding on every measurable indicator. Poverty, unemployment, and welfare budgets fell sharply, while satisfaction among former benefits claimants soared.

It is true that the 1996 act was passed at a time of strong economic growth, but this alone does not explain the almost miraculous shift from dependency to gainful work. The number of families on welfare fell from 5 million to 2 million; 1.6 million children were taken out of poverty. And perhaps most impressive, the reforms lifted groups who had been untouched by every previous welfare initiative: Poverty among black children fell from 42 to 33 percent; among single mothers from 50 to 42 percent.

So what was the magic formula? What wand did President Clinton wave to conjure so extraordinary a transformation? Essentially, he devolved responsibility. The 1996 Personal Responsibility and Work Opportunity Act shifted Social Security from the federal government to the states and gave local authorities incentives to reduce their caseloads. Offered the freedom to experiment, the states seized it with gusto. Some incentivized employers to take on the workless; others organized schemes themselves; most made the receipt of benefits conditional on taking up job offers. Best practice quickly spread as states copied what worked elsewhere.

At the same time, no state could afford to carry on as before, signing checks with a minimum of questions asked. Doing so would, as legislators well understood, make such a state a magnet for every bum in America. There was, in short, a measure of healthy competition.

It cannot be stressed too strongly that without U.S. federalism, the 1996 reforms couldn't have happened. Federalism did precisely what it was meant to do, ensuring benign competition.

For one thing, large bureaucracies create unintended consequences. Where states and counties can tailor their policies to suit local needs, a uniform system that covers 300 million people is bound to contain loopholes, tempting into dependency some who were never envisaged as claimants.

For another, proximity facilitates discernment. Person A may be a deserving widow who has been unlucky, while person B is a layabout. Local caseworkers may see this clearly. But if the universal rules handed down from Washington place the two applicants in the same category, they must be treated identically.

Third, pluralism spreads best practice. The freedom to innovate means that states can come up with ideas that Washington would never have dreamed of.

Fourth, non-state agents – churches, charities, businesses – are likelier to involve themselves in local projects than in national schemes, and such organizations are far better at taking people out of poverty than are government agencies.

Fifth, localism transforms attitudes. In Europe, many see benefit fraud as cheating "the system" rather than cheating their neighbors. People would take a very different attitude toward, say, the neighbor whom they knew to be claiming incapacity benefits while working as an electrician if they felt the impact in their local tax bill.

Finally, and perhaps most important, localism undergirds the notion of responsibility: our responsibility to support ourselves if we can, and our responsibility to those around us – not an abstract category of "the underprivileged," but visible neighbors – who, for whatever reason, cannot support themselves. No longer is our obligation discharged when we have paid our taxes. Localism, in short, makes us better citizens.

This is why it is such a pity to see that the 1996 legislation has now been eclipsed. In all the fuss about the stimulus package of February 2009, its most damaging provisions were barely reported. Under the guise of contingency, Washington has casually reassumed control of welfare spending. The reforms are over. America is drifting back to dependency.

In Europe, of course, the renationalization of benefits was seen as a return to humane values. European commentators tend to see state welfare as morally preferable to individual benevolence. The former allows poor people to claim an entitlement that is theirs by right. The latter demeans them by obliging them to take charity.

The European conception, of course, can easily descend into equating decency with high taxes. In consequence, private charity, in its widest sense, has been squeezed out. As the state has expanded, society has dwindled. Government officials – outreach workers, disability awareness counselors, diversity advisers, inspectors, regulators, licensors, clerks – have extended their jurisdiction. But they have done so at the expense of traditional authority figures: parents, school principals, clergy.

In assuming monopolistic responsibility for social policy, European states have balefully redefined how their citizens relate to one another. It wasn't so long ago that any adult, seeing a child out of school during term, would stop him and say, "Why aren't you in class?" Now this is seen as the state's duty. It wasn't so long ago that we all kept an eye out for elderly neighbors and looked to see that they were still collecting their milk bottles each morning. Now this too is seen as the government's responsibility.

The poor, in short, have been left to the Left – with calamitous consequences.

Europe Is Dying

The state has assumed control over functions that were once discharged within families: health, education, day care, provision for the elderly. So it is perhaps no surprise that the family itself is in decline in Europe.

I don't simply mean that the nuclear family has been replaced by a broader diversity of combinations. I mean that there are fewer and fewer babies. The current population of the continent, including European Russia, is around 720 million. According to a U.N. forecast, that figure will have fallen to 600 million by 2050. Germany's population will fall by 20 million, Russia's by 30 million – a far greater loss than was suffered as a consequence of the Nazi invasion and consequent deportations. The EU's own statistical office, Eurostat, tells a similar story. Within the next 50 years, it expects Germany's population to fall by 14 percent, Poland's by 18 – figures that include net immigration.

Albania is the only European country with what demographers call replacement-level fertility: 2.1 or more live births per woman. In every other European state, the population will decline except to the extent that it is off - set by immigration. This is not, unlike most forecasts, based on an extrapolation of current trends. The fall in births has already happened: It's a fact. All that remains for us is to decide how to deal with its consequences.

We can also, of course, speculate about its causes. Perhaps the babies are missing because of the spread of contraception and the legalization of abortion. Perhaps the decline has to do with lifestyle changes and the fact that women are settling down at a later age. Perhaps it is simply a function of choice or of a fashion for smaller units.

The one thing we can say definitively is

this: The problem is not nearly so severe in the U.S. The number of live births per American woman is almost exactly what demographers estimate to be the rate at which a population will remain stable: 2.1. In Europe, the figure is 1.5.

Can we connect these figures to politics? I think so. What Europeans most disdain in America, especially Red State America, is cultural conservatism. Even those who have little truck with anti-Americanism feel more or less obliged to sneer at America's Christian Right. But I can't help noticing that values voters seem to be keeping up their numbers. Just as the U.S. is outbreeding Europe, so the Republicans are outbreeding the Democrats. Megachurches may offend European taste, but they have plenty of children in their Sunday schools.

The higher rates of church attendance in the U.S. are arguably themselves a product of small government. The U.S. was founded on the basis that there would be no state church; instead, there would be friendly competition among congregations. In most of Europe, by contrast, there is either a single state church or a number of approved religious bodies, often in receipt of state funds. In other words, religion in the U.S. has been privatized: There is a free market of denominations. And privatization, as we know, tends to raise standards across the board. With no state support, American churches compete for worshipers, and worshipers compete to raise their ministers' salaries. At the same time, people tend to be more loyal to what they have chosen than to what they have been allocated.

European countries retain the outward forms of religion. Monarchs mark the key events of their reigns with religious services; bishops participate at state functions; but the cathedrals are empty.

Consider the chronology. The major expansion of government in Europe came during the Second World War; powers seized on a supposedly contingent basis during mobilization were generally retained when peace returned. Exactly a generation later, from about 1970, birthrates plummeted. The first generation raised with cradle-to-grave welfare, to be excused the traditional responsibilities of adulthood, was also the first to give up on parenthood. Throughout this period, there was a decline not only in church attendance but in the social values that traditional morality had encouraged.

I am not positing a sole and sequential link between these developments. Plainly, there are several factors at work, and we should be careful not to oversimplify. But we can say one thing with confidence: Europeans are extraordinarily relaxed about their continent's sterility. If the figures cited by the U.N. and Eurostat are even vaguely accurate, Europe faces a choice between depopulation and immigration on a scale never before seen. In a healthy polity, you'd expect there to be a lively debate about what to do next. But European voters have long since given up on politics as a means to deliver meaningful change. It's altogether more pleasant to talk about something else.

* * *

In Amsterdam on November 2, 2004, Mohammed Bouyeri, a 26-year-old Dutch Moroccan, shot Theo van Gogh, a filmmaker and professional pain in the neck, before methodically slicing him open with a machete. He then strolled calmly away, telling a screaming witness, "Now you know what you people can expect in the future."

The fact that Bouyeri, like the murderer of the populist politician Pim Fortuyn 18 months previously, had pedaled to the crime scene by bicycle gave the affair a grisly Dutch motif, but the controversy quickly became global.

Most European governments recognized the problem: They too had managed to alienate a minority of their second-generation immigrants and drive them into armed revolt.

During the past decade, dozens of young British men have traveled to Iraq and Afghanistan to take up arms against their fellow countrymen. At least two crossed from the Gaza Strip into Israel as suicide bombers.

Others have been involved in domestic terrorism, notably a bomb attempt on the London Underground.

So here's the question: Why is the problem so much less pronounced in the U.S.? There are more practitioners of Islam in America than in Britain, Belgium, and the Netherlands combined. While the U.S. doesn't keep religious census data, most estimates range between 2.5 million and 4.5 million, depending on how many devotees of the various African American Muslim movements established in the 20th century are considered orthodox.

If those who blame the disaffection of European Muslims on Western foreign policy were right, one would expect a similar disaffection among their American coreligionists. After all, if Britain is damned by radical mullahs for allying itself with the U.S., how much more terrible must be the Great Satan itself?

The U.S., of course, prides itself on its success in integrating newcomers. The country was, in a sense, designed for that purpose, and

American nationality has always been a civic rather than an ethnic or religious concept. It's a heartening creed and one to which immigrants from every continent have subscribed. As Ronald Reagan put it in a characteristically upbeat phrase, "Each immigrant makes America more American."

The U.S., in short, gives all its citizens, including its Muslim citizens, something to believe in. There is no need to cast around for an alternative identity when you are perfectly satisfied with the one on your passport.

In most of Europe, however, patriotism is seen as outdated and discreditable. The EU is built on the proposition that national identities are arbitrary, transient, and ultimately dangerous. Indeed, even the passports have been harmonized: the stiff blue British passport has been replaced by a floppy purple EU one. European countries make little effort to inculcate national loyalty in their immigrant communities, because they feel no such loyalty themselves. I am not speaking here of the general population but of the political and intellectual leaders who have systematically derided and traduced the concept of patriotism for the past 40 years.

The troubled young men who set out from Beeston and Wanstead and Tipton to become terrorists had been reared by the British welfare state. One might have thought that their great-grandfathers had greater cause to resent the United Kingdom that had, after all, invaded and occupied their homelands. But paradoxically, it was precisely this demonstration of power and confidence that facilitated their loyalty.

"Thou must eat the White Queen's meat, and all her foes are thine," Kipling's border chieftain tells his son. Compare that to the experience of a young Muslim growing up in one of Britain's inner cities. To the extent that he was taught any British history, it will have been presented to him as a hateful chronicle of racism and exploitation. Most of his interactions with the state will have taught him to despise it. Nor will he get much encouragement from his country's leaders. As British identity is scorned, the inhabitants of its constituent nations have begun to grope backward toward older patriotisms: Welsh, Scottish, or English. But where does this leave the children of immigrants?

Revolutionary violence historically has tended to occur, not at times of deprivation, but at times of rising wealth and aspiration.

The problem of disaffection is exacerbated by welfarism. Two of the London Tube bombers had been living on benefits, as many of the radical imams around Europe have always done. The idea that poverty is a breeding ground for violence and terrorism derives, ultimately, from Karl Marx, and like most of his teachings, it sounds plausible enough until you stop to analyze it. Revolutionary violence historically has tended to occur, not at times of deprivation, but at times of rising wealth and aspiration. Put bluntly, people who are worried about where the next meal is coming from have little time for protest marches, let alone bomb-making.

The modern welfare state, by contrast, is the ideal terrorist habitat. It keeps people fed but idle. And naturally, it makes them resent their paymasters.

BRITISH LIBERTY THRIVES IN AMERICA

The diverse Euro-woes identified in this Broadside gush from a single spout. All of them are caused, or at least exacerbated, by the phenomenon of large and remote government. Other things being equal, big and centralized states are likelier than small and devolved states to be sclerotic; have more bureaucrats and higher taxes; have soulless and inefficient welfare systems; crowd out non-state actors, from churches to families;

and have fatalistic and cynical electorates.

To put it the other way around, the devolution of power stimulates growth, makes administration more democratic, connects citizens with their nation, and allows a flourishing private sphere: the attribute that Tocqueville most admired about America.

Why is a European politician urging you to avoid Europeanization? Well, I'm not European; I'm British. I sometimes wish American conservatives would be a little bit more alive to the distinction. Being asked as a Briton how we're handling the Greek or Irish economic crises is rather like my asking you when you're going to vote against Hugo Chávez.

Britain is linked to the U.S., and to the wider Anglosphere, by ties of history and geography, commerce and law, blood and speech. Indeed, as a British politician, I see the American republic as a repository of our traditional freedoms. The political philosophy that became British liberalism and that found political expression in the common law, in the Magna Carta, and in the Bill of Rights found

[43]

its fullest and most sublime expression in the old courthouse of Philadelphia. Britain, as a result of its unhappy membership in the European Union, has now surrendered a large part of its birthright. But our freedoms live on in America.

I realize that this idea might sound strange to some American readers. After all, wasn't your country born in a popular rebellion against Britain? Didn't the patriot leaders define themselves against the British? Didn't Paul Revere rouse a nation with his cry of "The British are coming"?

Actually, no. If you think about it, that would have been a very strange thing to shout at people who had never considered themselves anything other than British. What Paul Revere actually cried was "The regulars are out!" The fighting that began the next day is best understood as a civil war fought within a common polity.

The ideas that animated the revolutionaries and that were eventually enshrined in the U.S. Constitution were all commonplaces in contemporary British politics. Most inhabitants of Great Britain would cheerfully have assented to the propositions that laws should be passed only by elected representatives; that taxes might not be levied save with the permission of the legislature; that no one should be subject to arbitrary punishment or confiscation; that ministers should be held to account by elected parliamentarians; that property rights should be defended by independent magistrates; and that there should be a separation between the executive, legislative, and judicial arms of the state.

American historians, quite understandably, tend to de-emphasize the extent to which Britain sympathized with the grievances of the colonists. They tend to gloss over the fact that several British officers refused their commissions and that William Howe, who eventually accepted the command (after three others had turned it down) did his duty to the letter, but no more. The truth was that most people in the mother country had no stomach for a war against their cousins who, as they saw it, were asserting the rights that all Britons ought to enjoy.

"If the ministry had succeeded in their first scheme on the liberties of America, the liberties of this country would have been at an end," Charles James Fox told the House of Commons in 1780.

Later accounts of the revolution generally portrayed it as a national uprising – as, indeed, a War of Independence. But this interpretation depends on a very selective reading of what the patriot leaders were arguing *at the time.* They saw themselves not as revolutionaries but as conservatives. In their own minds, all they were asking for was what they had always assumed to be their birthright as Englishmen. The real revolutionaries, as they saw it, were those in the Georgian Court who were seeking to impose a new settlement, in contravention of the ancient constitution: one that would tilt the balance from legislature to executive and open the door to oppressive government.

This brings me to my country's present tragedy. The fears that the American patriot leaders had about a Hanoverian tyranny were, in retrospect, exaggerated. The United Kingdom did not develop into an absolutist state. Power continued to pass from the Crown to the House of Commons. Indeed, many of the political developments that occurred in the U.S. happened in parallel in the United Kingdom, for the obvious reason that the two states were starting from a similar place.

The real divergence has come much more recently. It has come about as a result of a general shift in power in the United Kingdom from Parliament to standing bureaucracies, from local councils to central ministries, and, most damagingly, from Westminster to the EU. It is the process of European integration, above all, that has concentrated power in the hands of functionaries, in Whitehall as well as in Brussels.

In consequence, the grievances that the Americans laid against George III are now, more than two centuries later, coming to pass in earnest. Colossal sums are being commandeered by the government in order to fund bailouts and nationalizations without any proper parliamentary authorization. Legislation happens increasingly through what are called standing orders, a device that allows ministers to make laws without parliamentary consent – often for the purpose of implementing EU standards. Elections have been drained of purpose, and turnout is falling. Local councils have surrendered their prerogatives to the central *apparat*. Foreign treaties are signed by the prime minister under what is known as Crown prerogative, meaning that there is no need for parliamentary approval. Appointments to the growing corpus of state functionaries are made in the same way.

How aptly the British people might today apply the ringing phrases of the Declaration of Independence against their own rulers, who have "combined with others to subject us to a jurisdiction foreign to our constitution, and unacknowledged by our laws."

Throughout my career in politics, I have campaigned to apply Jeffersonian democracy to British political conditions, to recover those British freedoms that have flourished more happily in America than in their native soil, to repatriate our revolution. So you can imagine how I feel when I see the U.S. making the same mistakes that Britain has made: expanding its government, regulating private commerce, centralizing its jurisdiction, breaking the link between taxation and representation, abandoning its sovereignty.

You deserve better, cousins. And we expect better.

First American edition published in 2011 by Encounter Books, an activity of Encounter for Culture and Education, Inc., a nonprofit, tax exempt corporation.
Encounter Books website address: www.encounterbooks.com

Manufactured in the United States and printed on acid-free paper. The paper used in this publication meets the minimum requirements of ANSI/NISO z39.48–1992 (R 1997) (*Permanence of Paper*).

FIRST AMERICAN EDITION

LIBRARY OF CONGRESS CATALOGING-IN-PUBLICATION DATA

Hannan, Daniel.
Why America must not follow Europe / by Daniel Hannan.
p.   cm. — (Encounter broadsides)
ISBN-13: 978-1-59403-560-9 (pbk. : alk. paper)
ISBN-10: 1-59403-560-1 (pbk. : alk. paper)
1. United States—Politics and government—2009– 2. United States—Economic policy—2009– 3. United States—Social policy—1993– 4. Obama, Barack. 5. European Union countries—Politics and government. 6. European Union countries—Economic policy. 7. European Union countries—Social policy. I. Title.
JK275.H36 2011
320.60973—dc22
2010053557

10 9 8 7 6 5 4 3 2 1